The Cooking Book

Jane Bull

A Dorling Kindersley Book

A Penguin Company
LONDON, NEW YORK, MUNICH, PARIS,
MELBOURNE, AND DELHI

DESIGN • Jane Bull
TEXT • Penelope York
PHOTOGRAPHY • Andy Crawford
DESIGN ASSISTANCE • Laura Roberts

MANAGING EDITOR • Sue Leonard
MANAGING ART EDITOR • Cathy Chesson
PRODUCTION • Shivani Pandey
DTP DESIGNER • Almudena Díaz

For my cookery teacher Barbara Owen
(who's also my mother)

First published in Great Britain in 2002 by
Dorling Kindersley Limited
80 Strand,
London WC2R 0RL

2 4 6 8 10 9 7 5 3

Stir up something tasty

A CIP catalogue record for this book
is available from the British Library

ISBN: 0-7513-1478-1

Colour reproduction by
GRB Editrice S.r.l., Verona, Italy
Printed and bound in Italy by L.E.G.O.

See our complete
catalogue at
www.dk.com

what's cooking in this book..?

delicious dishes and

tantalizing treats!

Getting Started

Follow this advice before you begin and you will find the recipes much easier and safer. But most importantly ENJOY IT!

Safety first
Taking care in the kitchen

You should always tell an adult what you are up to in the kitchen so they can be around to help you.

⭐ Warning star

Watch out! The kitchen can be a dangerous place unless you are careful and use tools properly. When you see this symbol it means that something is hot, sharp, or electric, and so you will need to ask an adult to give you a hand.

It's hot!

⭐ Ask an Adult
When you see this sign it means that you need adult help.

Hot ovens and steaming pans

Always wear oven gloves when you are using the oven, let hot food stand to cool, and beware of hot steam.

Electric tools

It's electric!

Make sure you have an adult with you when you are using electrical items. Your hands should be dry when you use them and always unplug them when finished.

Sharp knives

It's sharp!

Watch your fingers when you slice and NEVER walk around carrying a knife.

Kitchen rules ok

It makes sense to keep a kitchen clean and tidy when you're cooking; so here are some tips.

Cover up Wear an apron or old shirt

Wash up Scrub your hands clean

Tidy up as you go along

All set? Off you g[o]

weights and measures

Weigh out your ingredients before you start, that way you won't leave anything out.

weighing time

For dry ingredients use weighing scales. For liquids use a measuring jug. REMEMBER if you start a recipe using grams then stick to them. Don't mix up grams and ounces in one recipe.

WEIGHING SCALES

A spoonful

In this book a spoonful is flat on top, not rounded. Try using a measuring spoon, they have standard sizes from a tablespoon right down to $1/2$ a teaspoon.

Look out for these abbreviations in the recipes:
tbsp = tablespoon
tsp = teaspoon

MEASURING JUG

MEASURING SPOONS

How much will it make?

This symbol will tell you how much the recipe will make, for example, "makes 12 cakes".

How long will it take?

When you see this little clock symbol in a recipe, it tells you how long the meal or snack will take to cook.

Food facts

Food is amazing stuff – it tastes good and is fun to play with; but the best thing about it is it keeps you alive. Your body needs different foods to keep you well and happy. Here are a few types.

Body builders

These are proteins. You can find proteins in meat, eggs, milk, cheese, and beans. They help your body to grow and make muscles strong.

Bug busters

Vitamin C is found in fruit and vegetables, especially in kiwi fruit, oranges, and lemons. Vitamin C helps your body to fight off infections like colds and flu. You should eat at least five pieces of fruit and veg a day.

Energy foods

Energy foods are called carbohydrates. You get them from pasta, rice, bread, and sugary foods. They give your body energy. So if you're running around and doing sport they will help you to go on for longer.

Treats and sweets

Sugary foods that taste really good give you short bursts of energy that don't last very long. However, even though sweets, chocolates, and sticky buns taste good, they are not good to eat all the time.

I want to grow up big and strong

your cooking kit

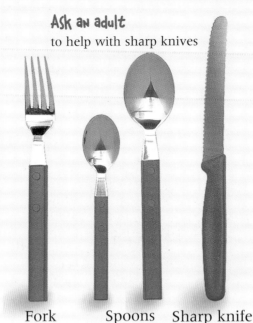

Ask an adult
to help with sharp knives

Fork   Spoons   Sharp knife   Wooden spoon   Spatula

Here are the tools used in this book

It's always best to collect up the tools you need before you start cooking.

Large mixing bowl

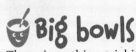

Small bowl

Big bowls

There is nothing trickier than having to mix too much in a small bowl. Always choose one that can fit double your mixture

Hand blender

Ask an adult
to plug in the electrical gadgets

Electric tools

Electrical tools are very useful – they help with all of those jobs that make your arm tired. But if you don't have them it's not the end of the world, you'll just have to mix by hand!

Blender

Electric whisk

6

Rolling-pin

Pastry cutters

Sieve

Pastry brush

Chopping board

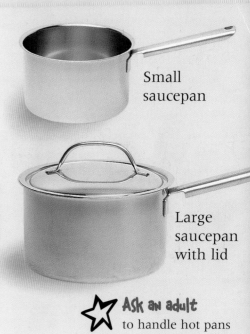

Small saucepan

Large saucepan with lid

☆ Ask an adult to handle hot pans

20 cm (8 in) cake tin

20 cm (8 in) cake tin with loose base

Bun tin and paper cake cases

Baking tray

Foil

Clingfilm

Cooling rack

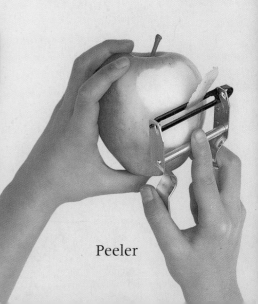

Peeler

Play dough

Have fun with bread dough: squeeze and shape it, watch it grow – then eat it hot from the oven.

To make your dough collect these ingredients

7 g (1 sachet) easy blend yeast

750 g (1½ lb) strong white flour

450 ml (¾ pint) warm water

1 tsp salt

2 tsp sunflower oil

Makes about 10 plain rolls

Shine up your shapes by brushing them with beaten egg

To decorate your dough

1 beaten egg

Sunflower seeds

Poppy seeds

Currants and raisins

8

1. Mix it all up

Put the yeast, flour, warm water, salt, and oil into a bowl and mix them together.

2. Take the mixture out

Sprinkle the worktop with flour and take the mixture out of the bowl.

3. Start kneading

To knead, press your fist hard into the dough, then turn it and do it aga[i]

How to make play dough

Have some fun playing with your bread dough. You'll really love to squeeze it. Squish it around, roll it into shapes, then decorate it by making a whole bread family. Watch it grow and when it's baked, serve it up hot with butter. Yum!

7. Place on a greased tray

Make sure you place the shapes far apart from each other.

8. Leave them to rise

Cover the tray loosely with clingfilm and leave it in a warm place. Leave it until it's double its size – about 30 min[

4. Keep kneading

Knead for 10 minutes
The dough should be stretchy, not sticky.

5. Cut up the dough

Divide the dough into smaller pieces or pull off chunks to play with.

6. Have a play

Choose a design – try making faces.

⭐ Set the oven to 220°C/425°F/Gas mark 7

PLAY DOUGH TOOLS

MIXING BOWL

WOODEN SPOON

PASTRY BRUSH

CLINGFILM

KNIFE

BAKING TRAY

COOLING RACK

9. Brush on egg and decorate

Brush the bread with beaten egg and decorate with seeds.

11. Bake your bread

⭐ Bake for 10-15 minutes. The small shapes will cook quicker, so take them out sooner.

Popcorn *

Pop *pop* Pop * Have a *Pop* at making Pop corn. But keep the Pop lid on, or it'll Pop everywhere!

1 tbsp oil

60 g (2 oz) popping corn

60 g (2 oz) butter

Makes one big bowlful

Sweet or Salty

Sprinkle sugar or salt over your popcorn while it is still in the pan.

TOOLS FOR *Pop* POPCORN

SAUCEPAN WITH LID

WOODEN SPOON

12

Let the oil get really hot

1. Heat up the oil and pop in the corn

⭐ Ask an adult to help with the very hot pan.

pop*

*pop *pop

When they stop popping, give the pan a shake.

2. Pop on the lid listen out for pops

🕐 Cook for about a minute, or until there are no more pops.

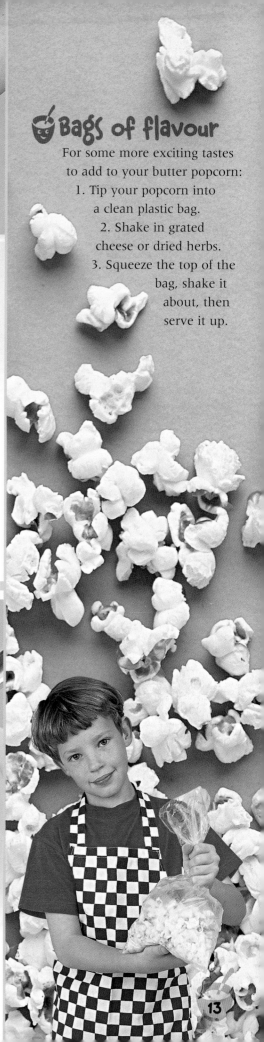

🍹 Bags of flavour

For some more exciting tastes to add to your butter popcorn:
1. Tip your popcorn into a clean plastic bag.
2. Shake in grated cheese or dried herbs.
3. Squeeze the top of the bag, shake it about, then serve it up.

Take it off the hob to cool it down

3. Turn off the heat and take a peak

You won't need any heat under the pan

4. Stir in the butter, it's ready to eat

13

Pick and mix Soup

make up

Try making it green or orange, smooth or chunky, but most of

Cook this mix up for starters

Makes about two big bowls or ten tiny ones

Knob of butter

Onion

Red pepper

Apple

Carrot

600 ml (1 pint) water

Stock cube

Mixed herbs

14

your own recipe
sweet or savoury,
mild or spicy –
all, make it
tasty

what did the big MUG
say to the little MUG?

eat up, and soon
you'll be as big as me!

Stir up Some Soup

Chop Chop Chop

Get souped-up to make this yummy starter. All it takes is lots and lots of chopping. Cut the vegetables into small pieces and the rest of it is simple.

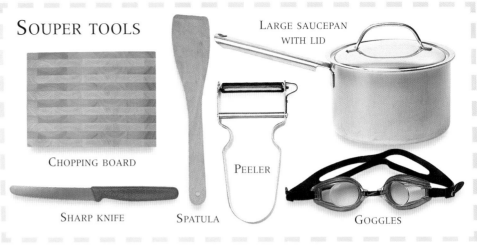

SOUPER TOOLS

CHOPPING BOARD

SHARP KNIFE

SPATULA

PEELER

LARGE SAUCEPAN WITH LID

GOGGLES

No more tears if you chop the onions with goggles on

★ Ask an adult to help with sharp knives

Chop off the top and the bottom, then pull off the skin

1. Melt the butter
in the saucepan over a low heat.

2. Add the onions
keeping the heat low so that they don't burn.

3. Cook Slowly
for about a minute until the onions look see-through and soft.

4. Add the rest

i.e. the chopped apple pepper, and carrot.

Slice, dice, and chop...

Keep your fingertips tucked away

The smaller the pieces, the quicker the soup will cook.

...and they're ready for the pot

Remove the seeds, pips, pith, and peel

A Smooth Soup

If you don't like lumpy soup, use a blender until it is smooth. LET THE SOUP COOL before you start blending.

Ask an adult to help you use a blender

5. Pour in the water and seasonings i.e. the herbs and stock cube.

6. Let it boil for a minute by turning up the heat.

Cook for 30 minutes

Watch out, the steam is HOT!

7. Gently Simmer Turn the heat down and simmer for 30 minutes over a low heat.

Souper! It's ready to eat

8. Check the Soup After cooking check that everything is cooked.

Perfect pasta

1. Boil some water
When the water is bubbling, add the pasta.

⭐ Ask an adult to help with the hot water

2. Cook the pasta
Keep boiling for about 10 mins or follow instructions on the packet.

3. Drain the water away through the sieve
Rest the sieve on the saucepan. Now it's ready to serve up.

Tomato sauce

1. Heat the oil
Peal and chop the garlic; then fry it in the saucepan.

2. Add tomatoes
⭐ Ask an adult to help as the oil will get hot.

3. Let it simmer
Add the herbs and sugar and stir. Let it simmer for 2 minutes.

Choose your pasta

125 g (4 oz) any quick cook pasta

600 ml (1 pint) water

Tomato Sauce

1 small tin of chopped tomatoes

1 tbsp olive oil

1 clove garlic

1 tsp sugar 1 tsp herbs

TOOLS FOR PASTA

SMALL SAUCEPAN FOR PASTA AND SAUCE

SIEVE

SPATULA

Quick cook pasta

Try out all sorts of shapes and sizes

Pasta

cook up a quick meal

of pasta with a tasty tomato sauce

Dish up dinner

When the sauce is ready, spoon it over the pasta and stir it up. Chop up some fresh herbs, such as basil leaves, for decoration and grate some cheese for extra taste.

Makes 2 helpings

flour
175 g (6 oz) plain flour

butter
90 g (3 oz)

water
About 6 tsp

red jam
125 g (4 oz)

Gem tarts and cheesy flans

Sweet or Savoury – these tarts can be both. A jammy teatime treat or a cheesy mini-meal. Pop them into your lunchbox as delicious snacks.

🥄 Shortcrust pastry

Once you know how to make this
pastry, you'll find that you can make
lots of dishes. You can make apple pies,
mince pies, sausage rolls, bigger flans
and quiches and much more.

= a gem tart **×**

Roll out the gem tarts

When you make the shortcrust pastry it is essential that you don't put in too much water, add a little at a time. Succeed with your tarts and you can call yourself a professional pastry chef! Experiment with fillings and test them on your family.

GEM TART TOOLS

LARGE MIXING BOWL   COOLING RACK   BUN TIN

SPOON   7.5 CM (3 IN) PASTRY CUTTER   ROLLING-PIN

Try these savoury cheese tarts

Collect up

Shortcrust pastry – the same as the gem tarts
2 eggs
60 g (2 oz) grated cheese
150 ml (1/4 pint) milk

1. Prepare the pastry in the same way as for the gem tarts.
2. Beat up the eggs in a bowl. Add the grated cheese and milk.
3. Spoon the mixture into the pastry cases.
4. Bake them in the same way as the gem tarts.

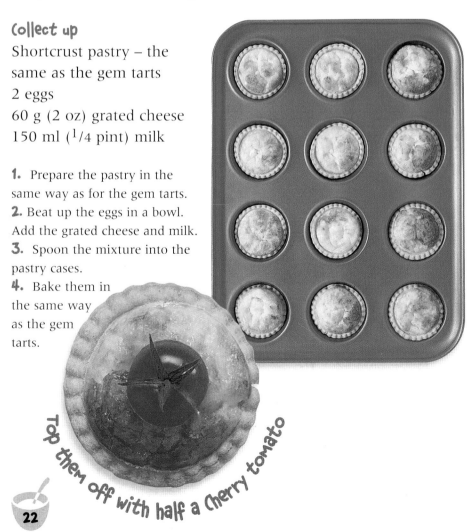

Top them off with half a cherry tomato

1. Rub together
the flour and butter with your fingers

5. Make a ball of pastry
The bowl will be clean when it's ready

9. Cut the cases
The bits left over can be shaped and cooked

2. Keep rubbing
until the mixture looks like breadcrumbs.

3. Add some water
Add six teaspoons to the mixture.

4. Squeeze it
Bring the mixture together into a ball.

6. Sprinkle flour
over the ball, rolling pin, and the table.

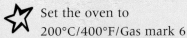

★ Set the oven to
200°C/400°F/Gas mark 6

Turn the pastry as you roll it.
Add flour to the table if it sticks.

7. Press down the ball

It should be about
4 mm (1/8 in) thick.

8. Start rolling

10. Spoon in the filling
Only half fill the cases with jam.

11. Bake the tarts
  Bake in the oven for
about 15 minutes

Royal tarts
for the queen
of hearts

Leave them to cool – if you can wait!

Moon rocks

Your mission – to reconstruct moon rocks that are good enough to eat. Read the scientific data carefully and report back at teatime.

This is what moon rocks are made of

One pinch of salt.

250 g (8 oz) self-raising flour	90 g (3 oz) soft brown sugar	90 g (3 oz) butter	125 g (4 oz) raisins	1/2 teaspoon mixed spice	1 egg

Collect these samples together, then turn the page to receive your instructions for moon rock construction

 Makes 8-12 moon rocks

One small step for man, one giant heap of cake for me!

Other space rocks to find

Leave out the raisins and try out these other tasty rocks.

Comet cocktail

125 g (4 oz) chocolate chips

Meteor shower

125 g (4 oz) sugar strands

Mars attack

Add 1 tsp of red food colouring at the same time as the egg.

MISSION MOON ROCK

Collect up your samples and prepare your work area.
* Check the tools and follow these instructions to proceed.
* Remember captain, you must be back from a successful mission in time for tea.
GOOD LUCK.

MISSION EQUIPMENT

MIXING BOWL

FORK

BAKING TRAY

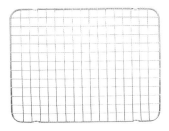

COOLING RACK

1. Throw in the butter and flour

Rub it between your fingers and thumbs until it looks like breadcrumbs.

2. Add the Sugar and raisins

Mix them up evenly using your han_
Add the mixed spice as well.

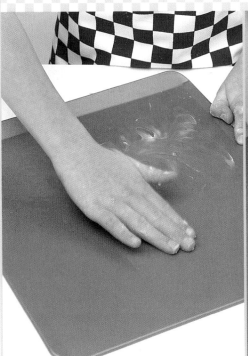

6. Grease the tray

Spread some butter over the tray.

 Set the oven to 200°C/400°F/Gas mark 6

7. Form rocky hea_

Make about 8-12 heaps, keeping th_
quite rough. Then put them in the _

3. Beat the egg in a separate bowl

Then add the beaten egg to the mixture.

4. Mix it together with a fork

Make sure it is all mixed up properly.

5. Stick your hand in and squeeze

Collect up all the bits in the bowl and squeeze them together into a ball.

8. Bake them ✫

Bake in the oven for about 15 minutes

Yummy! A successful mission, captain

Leave them to cool on a rack.

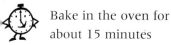

27

Mix up a mud pie

Load'em up! Move in the trucks to collect the materials for your mud pie. This is a mix that you don't even need to bake – IT'S SO EASY!

Chocolate strands

1 chocolate bar for topping

125 g (4 oz) castor sugar

warning! Mud Pie under construction

1 tbsp cocoa powder

175 g (6 oz) butter

125 g (4 oz) mixed dried fruit

250 g (8 oz) broken biscuits

Drive up and drop on some chocolate strands

Makes about
12 slices

Check out this slice

Mixing the mud

Shovel up all of the muddy ingredients in a saucepan, pack the earth down hard into the tin, pop into the fridge, and tip it out when it's ready. Add more mud and serve.

1. Melt the butter
⭐ Don't get it too hot, just melt it!

TOOLS TO MIX THE MUD

SAUCEPAN   KNIFE   WOODEN SPOON   20 CM (8 IN) DIAMETER CAKE TIN   FOIL

Try these mini mud pies

Finish the mini-pies with some gungy mud topping and some jelly creepy-crawlies

* Mix up the mud – the same way as for the big pie.
* Put some paper cake cases in a bun tin and divide the mud up equally.
* Place in the fridge to set.

5. Put foil in the tin

wheel out those pies! Vroom Yum

Makes about 12 mini-pies

How to make the Muddy topping

* Pour some very hot water into a bowl and place another bowl on top of it.
* Break up the chocolate and place it in the top bowl.
* Let the heat melt it.

⭐ **Ask an adult** to help with the hot water

2. Add cocoa and sugar
Take the pan off the heat to do this.

3. Now add fruit and biscuits

4. Mix it all up

6. Pour in the mix

7. Press it down

8. Place it in the fridge
Leave it for about 2 hours.

The steam will melt the chocolate.

Put the bowl of chocolate on top of a bowl of hot water

1. Melt the chocolate

2. Pour it on

3. Spread it out

Rainbow cakes

Heaps of colourful rainbow cakes cover the party table. Bake little cakes and decorate them however you like. Add your own fairy cake magic!

Magic up some fairy cakes
A measure, a whisk, or the swish of a wand.

125 g (4 oz)
self-raising flour

125 g (4 oz)
butter (room
temperature)

125 g (4 oz)
castor sugar

1 tsp baking powder

2 eggs

1 tsp vanilla essence

Makes 24 little cakes

LITTLE CAKE UTENSILS

MIXING BOWL

TEASPOON

TABLESPOON

SIEVE

COOLING RACK

ELECTRIC WHISK

Fill them
with paper
cake cases

2 BUN TINS

Rainbow icing

Mix up lots of little bowls of different coloured icing.
For green icing, mix yellow and blue; for orange,
mix yellow and red. Use anything sweet to decorate
the tops, such as glacé cherries, raisins, sweets, etc.

To ice 4 cakes

1 tbsp icing sugar
1 tsp water
1 drop food colouring

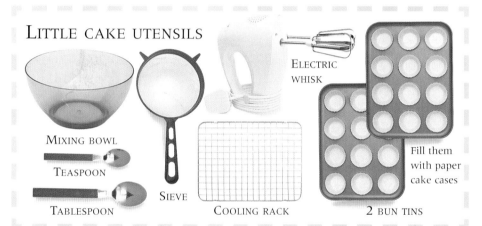

1. Stir together the water, food colouring, and icing sugar.

2. Drop a small dollop of icing into the centre of the cake and let it spread.

3. Decorate it with anything sweet, and use tubes of writing icing for extra patterns.

Sieving adds more air

1. Sieve the flour and baking powder
Set the oven to 190°C/375°F/Gas mark

5. Fill up the cases
Put a teaspoon of mixture in each case
Bake in the oven for 20 minutes.

3. whisk until it's creamy

2. Add everything else

Beat the eggs and throw them in with the butter, sugar, and vanilla essence.

4. Does it drop off a spoon?

If it drops off easily in a dollop, then it's ready.

6. Take out of the oven

⭐ **Ask an adult** to help with the hot oven.

Shhh... cakes cooling

upside-down

Looks like a cake, but turn it over and it's a fruity pudding!

125 g (4 oz) self-raising flour

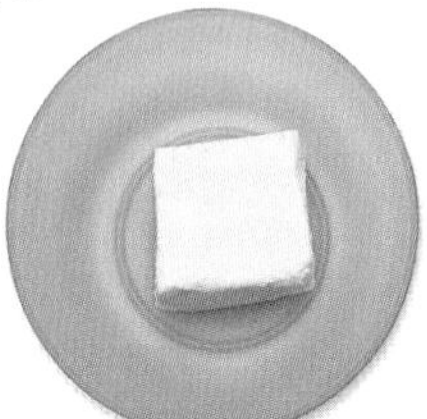

125 g (4 oz) butter

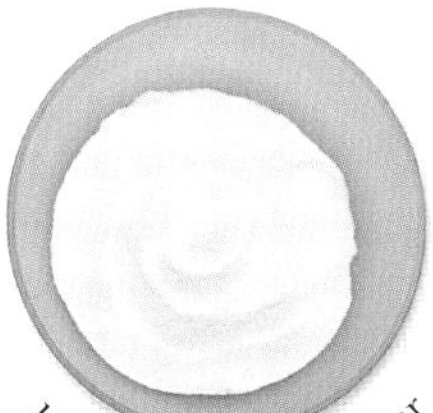

125 g (4 oz) castor sugar

2 eggs (beaten)

1 tsp baking powder

1 tsp vanilla essence

Hidden fruits to try: raisins, glacé cherries, tinned mandarin oranges, peaches, pineapple, apricots, or angelica

pudding

Mini upside-down puddings

Serve up your pudding hot and steaming with ice cream

Makes one big pudding or 24 small ones

37

Turn a pudding upside-down!

All you do is make the cake back to front – start with the top and end with the bottom! For mini upside-down puddings, use a bun tin with individual portions. Have fun doing it the wrong way around!

Sieve the flour

1. Put all of the cake ingredients in a bowl

UPSIDE-DOWN TOOLS

ELECTRIC WHISK

LARGE MIXING BOWL

SIEVE

20 CM (8 IN) DIAMETER CAKE TIN WITH LOOSE BASE

LARGE SPOON

KNIFE

SERVING PLATE

BUN TIN FOR MINI PUDDINGS

4. Arrange the fruit

Lay the fruit face side down so the pudding looks better at the end

9. Now flip it over

Using oven gloves, put one hand on each side.

8. Cover with a plate

It's ready when it falls
easily off the spoon
in a dollop.

2. whisk it until it's creamy

3. Grease the tin

⭐ Set the oven to
190°C/375°F/Gas mark 5

5. Spoon on the mixture

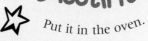

6. Smooth it out

⭐ Put it in the oven.

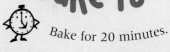

7. Bake it

🕐 Bake for 20 minutes.

10. Slide off the tin

Careful, it's hot! ⭐

Cool fruit

Eat us just the way we are,

or mix us into smooth fruit cocktails then freeze us for super cool lollies.

we're better than fast food – we're instant

Captain C

Vitamin C is great for helping your body to fight off colds and infections. You'll find vitamin C in all fruit and vegetables, especially when they are raw. So if you want to stay healthy then feast on fruit and gobble up your greens.

Squeeze me!

I'll add zest to anything

The big freeze
Very cool fruit lollies

Mix up your fruit drink, pour it into some lolly moulds, and pop them into the freezer. Drink any juice left over.

Banana and apple Slurp

1 banana
1 apple
450 ml (3/4 pint) milk
1 tbsp yoghurt
Prepare the fruit, whiz it up, and serve. Sweeten to taste.

Strawberries and cream

125 g (4 oz) strawberries
150 ml (1/4 pint) milk
150 ml (1/4 pint) cream
Prepare the fruit, blend it, and serve. Add extra sugar to sweeten it up.

Kiwi

Grape

Banana

Strawberry

Apple

Five fruit cup
Just chop up and fill a glass for an instant snack

Cream of kiwi

2 Kiwis
450 ml (3/4 pint) milk
Prepare the fruit, whiz it around, and serve. Add sugar or honey to sweeten.

How to make smooth fruit Slurps

Try out different varieties of fruit

Fresh fruit is the best if you can find it easily. If not, frozen or tinned fruit and its juice is good too. To prepare the fruit, remove the stalks and peel – you want to make your drink as smooth as possible so the less bits the better.

⭐ **Ask an adult** to help with the blender and the sharp knife.

TOOLS FOR SMOOTHING THE FRUIT

BLENDER OR HAND BLENDER ⭐

CHOPPING BOARD

SHARP KNIFE ⭐

To make a pink drink

😊 Makes 2 smooth glasses

90 g (3 oz) strawberries
1 banana
60 g (2 oz) raspberries
450 ml (^{3}/4 pint) milk
1 scoop ice cream
Sweeten to taste

1. Prepare the fruit ⭐

2. Drop in the fruit

⭐ **Ask an adult** to help with the blender.

INVENTING your own Slurp

There are so many ways to make your own, original fruit smoothies. You just have to experiment. Try adding some of these ingredients with the fruit. A good way to do it is to add a little at a time and keeping tasting. If your drink isn't sweet enough add a spoonful of sugar or honey.

Sugar or honey to sweeten

Don't forget to squeeze me – I'm tangy

Lemon juice

Water or fruit juice

Milk or cream – in small amounts

Your favourite flavour of ice cream

Plain or fruit yoghurt

3. Add the rest
Throw in the milk, ice cream, and sugar.

4. Screw the lid on tight
Whiz it up for 40 seconds.

Now pour it out and slurp away ahh... delicious

Savoury Snackpots

Vegetable sticks and your home-made breadsticks for dipping.

Hummus in a yoghurt pot is perfect for breadsticks.

Mix up some cream cheese and natural yoghurt to your taste.

Mixed nuts and dried fruit make a good titbit.

Pit-Stop Snacks

Ready Steady go!

Just like a motor car, you need filling up with fuel too! Brrrrmmmmm.

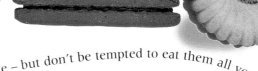

A candy car

For a quick power boost, I go well for a short distance

Display the sweets on a plate – but don't be tempted to eat them all yourself!

Try a wheel change

Chop up some fruit and make bike pictures. Wheel in the vitamin C.

Sweet Snackpots

Cut fruit sticks and slices for dipping or eating on their own.

Mix together some cream cheese and fruit yoghurt for a fruit dip.

Fill a pot to the brim with sweets. Squeeze as many in as you can.

Pop your home-made popcorn into pots for a quick snack.

Dips and Snackpots

Pit-stop snacks are perfect for parties or just when you need to refuel – load up a pot and munch away! Eat as much of the fruit and veg as you like but put the brakes on when it comes to the sweets!

weee...
...are full of energy

A veggy racer

I'm the winner! The veggies beat the sweets!

Chequered flag Sandwich

For the beginning and end of the race, rustle up a tasty chequered flag. Take two pieces of bread, one white and one dark brown, and spread them with cream cheese. Place the white over the brown and cut into squares. Arrange them as a flag.

Cooking words – greasing a tin

* rolling out * creaming * slicing * beating egg

Dough
This is the word for the thick, squishy flour mixture before it is cooked. It can be bread, biscuit, or pastry dough.

Kneading
Bread dough has to be kneaded, or turned and squashed a lot, to help spread the yeast throughout the dough.

Rising dough
After kneading the dough, it is left to rise, or sit for a while. This lets the yeast react, and the dough will grow to twice its size.

46

Boiling
This is when the heat is turned up high and whatever is in the pan bubbles busily. Mostly you only boil for a short time then let it simmer.

Simmering
Once the mixture has boiled, you can turn the heat down and let it simmer. This means letting the liquid bubble gently and steadily.

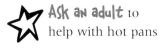

Ask an adult to help with hot pans

Breaking an egg
First tap the side of the egg hard on the rim of a bowl. Dig both of your thumbs into the hole you have made and prize the shell apart. Keep over the bowl at all times.

Beating eggs
Before adding eggs to ingredients, it's best to beat them first. Stir the eggs up very fast with a fork.

* chopping * boiling * Simmering * rubbing in
* Sifting * kneading * riSing

Here's a description of what they mean.

Rolling out

When you roll pastry dough, sprinkle flour on to the table and rolling pin before you start and keep sprinkling throughout to stop the dough sticking.

Chopping and Slicing

A recipe will tell you how big to chop or slice something. Always be careful when you use a knife.

Rubbing in

For biscuit, pastry, and crumble topping, the way to mix the flour and butter together is to rub them between your fingers and thumbs. Keep rubbing until the mixture looks like breadcrumbs.

Sifting

Sifting flour removes the lumps and adds air, which is good for making cakes. Gently tap the sieve against your hand to let it through.

Greasing a tin

To stop food sticking to a baking tray, smear a small amout of oil or butter all over the surface with your fingers. Get it right up to the edges.

Creaming

The cakes in this book use the one-stage method where the ingredients are all put together at the start. To cream, you beat this mixture until it falls off a spoon easily.

Ask an adult
to help with sharp knives

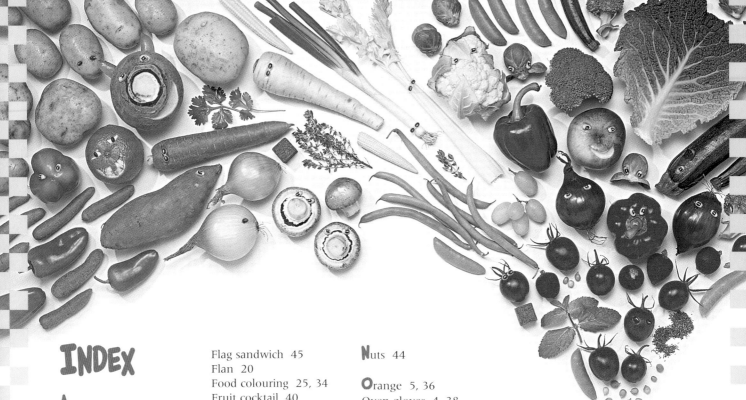

INDEX

ACKNOWLEDGEMENTS

With thanks to . . .
Maisie Armah, Charlotte Bull, Billy
Bull, James Bull,
Jackelyn Hansard, and Josephine
Hansard for being model cooks

All images © Dorling Kindersley.
For further information see:
www.dkimages.com